My Favourite Recipes

First printed 2010
Eaglemoss Publications Group, 1st Floor, Beaumont House,
Kensington Village, Avonmore Road,
London W14 8TS

ISSN 2043-0892
123456789

Reproduction by F E Burmans, UK.
Printed in the EU by Imprimerie Pollina.

My Favourite Recipes
Delicious Chicken
Front cover: Bono/Photocuisine (t), EM/Ken Field (bl), Jon Whittaker/Prima/NMC (br), 10 EM/Steve Lee (b), EM/Karl Adamson (t), 11 EM/Karl Adamson, 12 EM/Chris Alack (bl), EM/William Reavell (t), 13 EM/Graham Kirk (br), 15 Jon Whittaker/Prima/NMC, 17 EM/Ken Field, 19 Bono/Photocuisine, 21 Juliet Piddlington/Prima/NMC, 23 Jon Whittaker/Prima/NMC, 25 Jon Whittaker/Prima/NMC, 27 EM/Amanda Heywood, 29 Prima/NMC, 31 Duca/Photocuisine, 33 Jon Whittaker/Prima/NMC, 35 EM/Chris Alack, 37 EM/Steve Lee, 39 Richard Kolker/Prima/NMC, 41 Tim Winter/Prima/NMC, 43 Jon Whittaker/Prima/NMC, 45 Prima/NMC, 47 Liz Parsons/Prima/NMC, 49 EM/Ken Field, 51 Jon Whittaker/Prima/NMC, 53 Jon Whittaker/Prima/NMC, 55 Simon Smith/Prima/NMC, 57 Bagros/Photocuisine, 59 Roger Stowell/Prima/NMC, 61 Caste/Photocuisine, 63 Liz Parsons/Prima/NMC, 65 EM/Ken Field, 67 Tim Winter/Prima/NMC, 69 David Munns/Prima/NMC, 71 Jon Whittaker/Prima/NMC, 73 Gus Filgate/Prima/NMC, 75 Prima/NMC, 77 Prima/NMC, 79 Prima/NMC, 81 Geoff Fevey/Prima/NMC, 83 Rivère/Photocuisine, 85 Jon Whittaker/Prima/NMC, 87 Sean Myers/Prima/NMC, 88 Jon Whittaker/Prima/NMC, 91 Prima/NMC, 93 Liz Parsons/Prima/NMC.

EM = Eaglemoss Publications Group
NMC = The National Magazine Company

Delicious Chicken

My Favourite Recipes

Now, you'll never be stuck for inspiration at supper time with this fantastic new collection of chicken recipes. There's something for everyone, from quick and easy snacks and tasty salads to hearty pies and perfect roasts.

For most families, chicken is an essential part of their weekly diet and an economical choice for mealtimes. It's also an incredibly versatile ingredient that suits most cooking methods and combines well with hundreds of different flavours.

You can enjoy a roast chicken on Sunday, then use leftovers for curries, stir-fries, salads or pasta, and boil the carcass up to make a stock for soups and sauces – so there's no waste!

As well as the many tempting recipes in this book, there are loads of helpful tips and shortcuts to keep your cooking as simple and stress-free as possible.

Take a fresh look at chicken – these delicious recipes are sure to become favourites with all the family. I hope you enjoy them!

Becky Davis

Editor

My Favourite Recipes

Contents

Paprika Chicken

Warm Chicken & Potato Salad

Slow-cooked Chicken

Key to recipe symbols

Super Quick
Ready in under 15 minutes.

Quick
Ready in 30 minutes or less.

Make it at the Weekend
This dish needs a little more attention so make it when you have extra time to spare.

✓ *Easy*
Simple to prepare for most cooks.

✓✓ *Extra Easy*
Simple to prepare, even for an inexperienced cook.

Freeze it
This recipe can be frozen.

Spicy
This recipe has a bit of a kick!

N *Contains Nuts*
This recipe contains nuts.

V *Vegetarian*
This Recipe is suitable for vegetarians.

Inspiration, Tips & Ideas

Chicken is perfect for a huge range of recipes – from quick and easy snacks and stir-fries to roasts, salads, bakes and curries. Here are some tempting ideas to try plus tips for saving time and money to help you enjoy perfect poultry dishes.

Chicken is a real all-round favourite whether it's for the family supper or entertaining friends, plus it's easy to cook and incredibly versatile so there is sure to be a recipe to tempt your tastebuds, whatever the occasion.

COOKING TIPS

Chicken can be cooked in many different ways but some cuts suit some methods better than others. A whole chicken is best roasted or poached while smaller portions like legs and thighs can also be grilled, fried or barbecued. Boneless, skinless meat is best for stir-frying while portions with the bone still in are better for casseroles and stews as they retain more flavour and don't dry out so easily.

Cookery Secrets... Adapting a Recipe

MAKE IT EASY

- **If the chicken needs to be coated and marinated, buy flavoured chicken fillets instead, such as tikka, Mexican or barbecued.**
- **Reduce cooking times by using boneless chicken portions. Take care not to overcook or it will dry out.**
- **Buy a carton of fresh stock or use a good-quality powder or cube instead of making your own.**

IMPRESS WITHOUT STRESS

- **Mix soft butter with herbs, spices or lemon zest and push under the skin of a chicken before roasting.**
- **Serve a plain grilled chicken breast with a colourful salsa of mango, chilli, lime, red onion and avocado.**

SPEND LESS, EAT BETTER

Chicken can be an expensive choice, especially if you buy organic or free-range so look out for special offers and buy in bulk to stock up your freezer. Be creative with leftovers too – use the carcass of a roast chicken to make a stock for soups and stews. Use leftover cooked chicken meat for burgers, pies, stir-fries and soups (see our 3 meals from 1 chicken ideas opposite). Don't always go for chicken breasts, try cheaper cuts like thighs, drumsticks and wings.

USE YOUR FREEZER & STORECUPBOARD

Home-made stock can be frozen in ice cube trays and used as needed for casseroles, soups, stews and sauces. Alternatively turn the stock into a soup and freeze in portions

Make It Tonight... Ten Popular Chicken Recipes

- **Chicken tikka masala: chunks of spicy chicken in creamy tomato sauce.**
- **Chicken Caesar salad: lettuce, croûtons, Parmesan and creamy dressing.**
- **Coq au vin: French casserole with red wine, bacon lardons and shallots.**
- **Chicken & mushroom pie: creamy sauce topped with crisp puff pastry.**
- **Chicken soup: many versions, both creamy and clear; well known for its health-giving properties.**
- **Sweet & sour chicken: kids' favourite with pineapple, peppers and sauce.**
- **Southern fried chicken: coated in spiced breadcrumbs and deep-fried.**
- **Sticky chicken wings: great snack, coated in barbecue sauce and grilled.**
- **Chicken chow mein: noodles, veg, beansprouts and soy sauce.**
- **Chicken chasseur: rich tomato sauce.**

5 Ways with a Chicken Leg

- **Slash, stuff with sun-dried tomatoes and roast. Serve with cream sauce.**
- **Rub with Cajun seasoning and lime juice. Cook on the grill or barbecue.**
- **Coat in breadcrumbs mixed with paprika and thyme, drizzle with oil and bake until golden and cooked.**
- **Simmer in tomato pasta sauce with bacon and mushrooms for an easy stew.**
- **Coat with tomato ketchup, mango chutney, garlic, lemon juice, hot chilli sauce and a little oil and roast.**

for a quick and easy midweek meal. Keep a selection of shortcut ingredients in the cupboard so you can whip up a meal in minutes when time is short. Good products to go with chicken are curry pastes and sauces, canned coconut milk, canned tomatoes, soy sauce, chilli sauce, canned beans, mango chutney, pesto sauce, chilli powder and spice rubs. Look out for ready-made marinades too. They are a great, fuss-free way to flavour grilled or barbecued chicken.

Cookery Secrets... 3 Meals from 1 Chicken

Save money on the weekly shop with these simple suggestions to help you get 3 different meals from 1 chicken.

1 *Buy a large chicken and roast it for Sunday lunch. Serve with roast potatoes, stuffing and plenty of vegetables. When cool, strip all the leftover meat from the bones.*

2 *Mix most of the leftover meat with fried bacon, mushrooms, herbs and shallots in a red wine sauce. Spoon into individual pie dishes and top with a puff pastry lid. Bake until golden.*

3 *Boil the bones in water with onion, carrot and bay leaf to make stock. Strain. Add noodles, chilli, cabbage, onions and remaining leftover meat for a nourishing soup.*

Healthy Cooking

As well as being versatile and tasty, chicken is a healthy choice too. Here are some tips for lower-fat cooking that's still packed with flavour.

Chicken is a great ingredient to include in a healthy diet but the way you cook it and what you serve it with can make a big difference to the calories. Here are some simple ways to keep an eye on your waistline but still eat well.

HEALTH BENEFITS

Chicken is a good source of protein and also provides minerals such as calcium, zinc, potassium and iron, plus vitamins A and B. It also contains less saturated fat than red meats, especially if you remove the skin where most of the fat is found. Cooking chicken with the skin on does add flavour though so some recipes are best cooked like this and the skin removed before eating.

LOW-FAT COOKING

There are lots of easy ways you can replace ingredients or change cooking methods to reduce the fat in your favourite dishes. Chicken salad often seems a healthy option but watch out for the dressing and

Cookery Secrets... Low-fat Cooking Methods

- **Poaching uses no fat at all and is ideal for chicken portions or a whole bird. Cook in a pan of gently simmering water or stock. The meat should fall away from the bone easily.**

- **Steaming is another no-fat cooking method often used in Chinese cuisine. Place skinless chicken breasts in a steamer with flavourings such as ginger, lemon, garlic and herbs and cook over a pan of simmering water.**

- **Grilling or griddling is a good lower-fat cooking method, ideal for portions such as thighs and breasts. Brush the chicken with a little oil first or use a marinade. Baste regularly during cooking to stop it drying out.**

Healthy Substitutions to Reduce the Fat

- **Most of the fat in chicken comes from the skin so use skinless portions or remove the skin before eating.**
- **Avoid creamy sauces or use lower-fat replacements such as reduced-fat crème fraîche, natural yogurt or fromage frais.**
- **Stir-frying is a lower-fat way of cooking as you only need a little oil.**
- **White meat is the leanest cut so try and opt for chicken breasts or thighs.**
- **Don't deep-fry breaded chicken – spray with a little oil and bake in the oven instead.**

avoid fatty extras like crispy bacon or croûtons. Replace mayonnaise with natural yogurt or fromage frais in Coronation chicken, for example.

HEALTHIER CHOICES

When choosing a takeaway, go for healthier options like tandoori chicken or chicken tikka rather than those in creamy sauces like korma. Serve with sweet chilli sauce or a low-fat yogurt with chopped mint if you still want a creamy taste. If you opt for Chinese, choose a stir-fried dish like a chow mein rather than something deep-fried like sweet and sour chicken balls.

Makeover Recipe

Chicken in a White Wine Sauce

Serves 4
Original recipe 530 Kcals and 32.8g fat per portion
New version 282 Kcals and 6g fat per portion

700g (1½lb) skinless, boneless chicken breasts, each cut into 3–4 pieces
225g (8oz) button or pickling onions
600ml (1pt) chicken stock
150ml (¼pt) dry white wine
2 sprigs fresh thyme
2 tablespoons butter
2 tablespoons plain flour
225g (8oz) button mushrooms
150ml (¼pt) double cream
2 egg yolks
40g (1½oz) fried croûtons, to serve
Parsley, to garnish

1 Place the chicken, onions, stock, wine and thyme in a pan and bring to the boil. Simmer for 15 minutes. Remove chicken and onions. Boil the stock for 5 minutes then strain.
Poaching is a great low-fat cooking method. To cut cals further, replace half the stock and wine with water.

2 Melt the butter in a pan. Add the flour and cook, stirring for 1 minute. Stir in the poaching liquid. Cook for 5 minutes until smooth. Add the chicken, onions and mushrooms to the pan and cook for 3 minutes.
Replace the butter with low-fat spread and keep the heat low.

3 Mix egg yolks and cream then stir in. Cook gently for 2 minutes until thick. Serve with croûtons and parsley.
Omit the yolks and replace cream with low-fat yogurt. Cook very gently without boiling (the sauce will be thinner). Bake croûtons with a little spray oil instead of deep-frying.

Chicken Cuisine

Chicken is used in recipes all around the world, teamed with many different flavours so experiment and see where your supper will take you tonight.

From spicy Indian and Thai curries to Oriental stir-fries, Mediterranean stews and hearty British pies, chicken is used in cuisines all over the world. Whether you use a ready-made sauce or marinade or mix up your own ingredients, you can create an authentic tasting dish in your own home, which you can serve as a simple family supper or a more elegant dish for entertaining friends.

PERK UP YOUR POULTRY

An easy way to create a sensational supper is to use a ready-made seasoning mix or marinade. Simply add to chicken portions then bake, grill or fry for an easy but delicious supper. If you like a bit of heat, try Cajun spice mix rubbed over chicken breasts, then grilled and served with soured cream and salsa. Or marinate drumsticks or wings in peri-peri marinade then bake and serve with potato wedges. For a milder Oriental dish, coat sliced chicken breast in teriyaki marinade then stir-fry with spring onions and baby corn and serve with egg noodles. And barbecue marinade is great brushed over chicken thighs before grilling.

Jamaica

Jerked chicken wings

Jerk seasoning is a combination of sweet, sour, hot and spicy flavours

900g (2lb) chicken wings
3 tablespoons jerk seasoning
100ml (3½fl oz) red wine vinegar
2 tablespoons soy sauce
2 tablespoons vegetable oil

● Marinate the chicken wings in the seasoning, vinegar, soy and oil for at least 2 hours. ● Fry the wings in a little oil until browned then roast in a roasting tin at 200°C/400°F/Gas 6 for 10–15 minutes.

Chicken dopiaza

Dopiaza is made with two types of onion; here we use red onions and a ready-made sauce to save time

2 tablespoons vegetable oil
3 red onions, finely sliced
900g (2lb) skinless chicken breasts, cubed
350g jar dopiaza curry sauce
3 tablespoons each chopped fresh mint and coriander

● Heat the oil in a large pan and fry the onions over a medium heat for 5 minutes until softened. Add the chicken and fry for 3–4 minutes until browned on all sides.
● Pour over the sauce, cover and simmer for 20 minutes until the chicken is cooked. Add the coriander and mint and serve.

CREATE A CASSEROLE

A chicken casserole is a real crowd-pleaser and it's easy to give it an international flavour. Cook in red wine with mushrooms, shallots and bacon for a French-style stew or add tomatoes, peppers and basil for an Italian flavour. Use root veg and pearl barley for a Scottish twist or go Mexican with peppers, tomatoes and a little grated dark chocolate which adds a mellow richness.

FRUITY FLAVOURS

Chicken combines well with fruit too so cook with dried apricots and couscous for a taste of Morocco, team with mango and chilli for an Oriental treat or serve in a creamy wine sauce with green grapes for a classic French combination.

Mushroom Kievs

We update the Russian classic with a tasty Italian twist

4 chicken breasts with wing bones
15g (½oz) dried porcini mushrooms, soaked in water for 30 minutes
125g (4oz) softened butter
3 tablespoons chopped fresh chervil
1 teaspoon lemon zest and 2 teaspoons juice
Beaten egg and a mixture of ciabatta breadcrumbs and polenta, to coat

● Drain and chop the porcini. Mix with butter, chervil, zest and juice. Shape into 4 sausages and chill until solid. ● Cut off the chicken fillets then sandwich together with the butter 'sausages'. Press to seal in the butter completely. ● Dip the chicken in egg then the breadcrumbs to coat. Chill for 30 minutes. Coat again. ● Deep-fry at 160°C/310°F for 12 minutes until cooked.

✓ *Easy* ❄ *Freeze it*

Italian Herb Chicken

Preparation time 10 minutes ● Cooking time 1¼ hours

3 medium waxy potatoes, cut into large chunks
1 bulb garlic, broken into cloves, leaving skin intact
1 fennel bulb, roughly copped
2 tablespoons olive oil
4 large chicken legs
2 shallots, roughly chopped
6 plum tomatoes, roughly chopped
3–4 sprigs fresh thyme, leaves stripped and chopped
Salt and freshly ground black pepper
200ml (7fl oz) chicken stock

● **1** Preheat the oven to 190°C/375°F/Gas 5. Place the potatoes, garlic cloves and fennel in a pan of boiling water and cook for 10 minutes until the potatoes are just tender. Drain well and set aside.

● **2** In a large frying pan, heat the oil and cook the chicken legs over a medium heat, turning regularly, until golden all over. Transfer to a large ovenproof dish using a slotted spoon. Drain off the excess fat from the frying pan then add the shallots, tomatoes and thyme, season well with salt and freshly ground black pepper, and cook for 5 minutes, adding a splash of water if it looks too dry.

● **3** Add the potatoes, fennel and garlic to the chicken, then pour over the stock and tomato mixture. Cover and bake for 45–60 minutes until the chicken is golden and cooked through and the vegetables are tender.

Calories per portion 317 Kcal ● Fat per portion 12.4g ● Serves 4

Serve with...

This is a meal in itself – just serve with some warm ciabatta or garlic bread to mop up the delicious sauce.

Why not try...

You could use chicken thighs instead of legs if you prefer. Allow 2 thighs per person and reduce the baking time to 40–50 minutes.

Make it at the Weekend ❄ Freeze it

Chicken & Leek Pie

Preparation time 30 minutes ● Cooking time 1½ hours

15g (½oz) butter

6 skinless, boneless chicken breasts, cut into 2.5cm (1in) pieces

2 onions, diced

1 garlic clove, crushed

600ml (1pt) chicken stock

Salt and freshly ground black pepper

2 leeks, trimmed and cut into 2.5cm (1in) pieces

300ml (½pt) double cream

Squeeze of lemon juice

1 egg, lightly beaten, to glaze

350g (12oz) puff pastry

Serve with...

Serve the pie with a green vegetable, like mangetout, tossed with lemon zest.

- **Step 1** Melt the butter in a pan, add the chicken and cook for 2–3 minutes until white – don't let it brown. Add the onions and cook for 3–4 minutes. Add the garlic, stock and seasoning, bring to a simmer and cook for 15–20 minutes until the chicken is tender and cooked through.
- **2** Meanwhile, cook the leeks in a pan of boiling salted water for 2–3 minutes until just tender. Drain well and leave to cool.
- **Step 3** Transfer the chicken and onions to a bowl using a slotted spoon. Strain the stock into a clean pan then boil until reduced by two-thirds.
- **Step 4** Add the cream, bring to a simmer and cook for 10 minutes to make a thick coating sauce. Season and add a squeeze of lemon juice.
- **5** Add the chicken and leeks to the sauce. Pour into a 2ltr (3½pt) pie dish, reserving any leftover sauce to serve with the pie. Leave to cool.
- **6** Roll out the pastry and use to cover the pie. Score a pattern on top, make a hole in the centre, brush with egg and bake for 40 minutes until golden.

Calories per portion 675 Kcal ● Fat per portion 45.8g ● Serves 6

Step 1 *Heat the oil in a large, non-stick frying pan. Add the chicken and cook until white all over but not browned.*

Step 3 *Remove the chicken and onions from the stock using a slotted spoon and transfer to a bowl. Set aside.*

Step 4 *Cook the sauce for 10 minutes until reduced and thick enough to coat the back of the wooden spoon.*

✓ *Easy*

Moroccan Chicken Skewers

Preparation time 15 minutes + marinating ● Cooking time 10 minutes

½ teaspoon ground ginger
2 teaspoons paprika
½ teaspoon turmeric
Few strands saffron
2 garlic cloves, crushed
3 tablespoons chopped fresh coriander
1½ tablespoons lemon or lime juice
1½ tablespoons olive oil
Salt and freshly ground black pepper
700g (1½lbs) chicken breasts, cut into 2cm (¾in) cubes
6–8 lemons, cut into chunks
Fresh coriander sprigs, to garnish

● **1** Combine the ginger, paprika, turmeric, saffron, garlic, coriander, lemon or lime juice and olive oil in a large bowl. Season well with salt and pepper. Add the chicken and mix well to coat evenly. Cover and leave to marinate in the fridge for a few hours or overnight.

● **2** Preheat the grill or heat a griddle pan over a medium heat. Thread the chicken and lemons alternately onto skewers.

● **3** Cook the skewers under the grill or on the griddle for 5 minutes each side until the chicken is cooked through. Watch it carefully so it doesn't burn. Garnish with coriander and serve.

Calories per portion 130 Kcal ● Fat per portion 3.5g ● Serves 8

Serve with...

Serve the skewers with couscous and a yogurt and cucumber dip (tzatziki).

Why not try...

Preserved lemons are a popular Moroccan ingredient. If you can find a jar in the supermarket or a specialist food shop you could use them in this recipe instead of the regular lemons.

✓ *Easy*

Lemon Chicken Risotto

Preparation time 10 minutes ● Cooking time 25 minutes

700ml (1¼pts) chicken stock

250g (9oz) risotto rice

Low-fat cooking spray

4 medium boneless chicken breasts, cubed

Juice of 1 lemon and 2 tablespoons grated zest

60g (2½oz) Parmesan, grated

Freshly ground black pepper

- **1** Place half the stock in a pan with the risotto rice and bring to the boil. Simmer, stirring occasionally, until nearly all the stock has been absorbed. Add half the remaining stock and continue simmering, stirring occasionally.
- **2** Meanwhile, spray a non-stick frying pan with cooking spray and fry the chicken for 4–5 minutes until golden. Transfer to a plate and set aside.
- **3** When stock has been absorbed, add the lemon juice and zest to the rice. Add the remaining stock and the chicken pieces.
- **4** Simmer gently until nearly all the stock is absorbed and the rice is tender. Stir in the grated Parmesan, season with black pepper and serve.

Calories per portion 433 Kcal ● Fat per portion 7.5g ● Serves 4

Why not try...

Add some large cooked peeled prawns to the risotto just before the end of cooking and simmer until heated through.

Super Quick ✓✓ Extra Easy Spicy

Chicken Tikka Wraps

Preparation time 5 minutes ● Cooking time none

200g carton Greek yogurt

2 tablespoons roughly chopped fresh coriander

1 green chilli, chopped

Salt and freshly ground black pepper

4 tablespoons mango chutney

4 chapattis

2 x 210g packs chicken tikka fillets, chopped

100g (3½oz) baby spinach leaves

● **1** In a bowl, mix together the yogurt, chopped coriander and green chilli. Season with salt and freshly ground black pepper.

● **2** Spread the mango chutney on the chapattis and top with chicken tikka and spinach. Spoon over the yogurt dressing, then fold over and serve.

Calories per portion 342 Kcal ● Fat per portion 9.4g ● Serves 4

Why not try...

You can use other flavoured chicken fillets, such as barbecue or Mexican-style, instead of the tikka. Or use flour or corn tortillas instead of chapattis.

Quick ✓ Easy Spicy

Chicken Laksa

Preparation time 10 minutes ● Cooking time 15 minutes

1 tablespoon vegetable oil

2 tablespoons Thai red curry paste

1 stalk lemongrass, shredded

1 red chilli, cut into thin strips

4 skinless, boneless chicken breasts, cut into chunks

600ml (1pt) chicken stock

400g can coconut milk

125g (4oz) rice noodles

Zest of 2 limes

● **1** Heat the oil in a large saucepan and gently stir-fry the curry paste, lemongrass and three quarters of the chilli for 1–2 minutes. Add the chicken and continue to cook, stirring frequently, until golden all over.

● **2** Add the stock and coconut milk and bring to the boil. Simmer for 10 minutes until the chicken is cooked through.

● **3** Meanwhile, soak the noodles in boiling water for 4 minutes until soft, then drain and add to the chicken. Serve immediately, garnished with lime zest and the remaining chilli.

Calories per portion 458 Kcal ● Fat per portion 22g ● Serves 4

Serve with...

Simply add a sprinkling of fresh coriander and some lime wedges to squeeze over before eating.

Why not try...

For a vegetarian version, replace the chicken with sliced red pepper, baby corn and mushrooms. Use vegetable stock instead of chicken stock.

Make it at the Weekend ❄ Freeze it

Poached Chicken Casserole

Preparation time 15 minutes ● Cooking time 1 hour 40 minutes

Salt and freshly ground black pepper

1.3kg (3lb) oven-ready chicken, all excess fat trimmed off

3 onions, 1 halved, 2 diced

4 carrots, peeled, 3 diced

1 bay leaf

4 celery sticks, diced

1 large potato, diced

1 leek, diced

2 tablespoons frozen peas

25g (1oz) butter

85ml (3fl oz) single cream

Chopped fresh parsley, to garnish

Serve with...

A loaf of fresh crusty bread is all you need with this tasty casserole.

● **Step 1** Season the chicken and place in a pan with the halved onion, whole carrot and bay leaf. Cover with cold water. Bring to a simmer and skim off the froth from the surface with a slotted spoon. Cover and simmer for 1 hour. Remove the chicken and cool. Discard the vegetables and bay leaf.

● **2** Strain the stock, then skim off the excess fat from the surface with a spoon. Place the clear stock in a clean pan, add the diced onions, carrots, celery and potato. Bring to the boil then simmer for 20 minutes until tender.

● **Step 3** When the chicken is cool enough to handle, peel away and discard the skin. Break the chicken into joints and pull away the meat in strips.

● **4** Bring the stock to the boil and cook for 10 minutes until reduced. Add the leek and cook for 4 minutes. Add the peas and cook for 3 minutes.

● **Step 5** Add the butter and cream to pan, stirring well. Simmer for 2–3 minutes, or until the sauce thickens slightly. Add the chicken to the pan, warm through, then season, sprinkle with parsley and serve.

● Calories per portion 383 Kcal ● Fat per portion 17.9g ● Serves 4

Step 1 *Bring the water to a simmer then skim off and discard the froth from the surface using a slotted spoon.*

Step 3 *Remove the skin and pull the chicken meat away from the bones in strips – it should come away easily.*

Step 5 *Add the cream and butter to the pan, stirring well, until combined. Simmer until slightly thickened.*

✓ *Easy* ❄ *Freeze it*

Creamy Cider Chicken

Preparation time 10 minutes ● Cooking time 35 minutes

2 tablespoons olive oil

8 chicken portions

Salt and freshly ground black pepper

1 medium onion, finely chopped

1 eating apple, cored and cut into wedges

1 tablespoon plain flour

225ml (8fl oz) dry cider

150ml (¼pt) chicken stock

Few sprigs fresh thyme

1 bay leaf

1–2 tablespoons double cream

● **1** In a casserole dish, heat 1 tablespoon of oil. Season the chicken with salt and freshly ground black pepper and then cook until browned on all sides. Remove from the pan with a slotted spoon and set aside on a plate.

● **2** Drain off the excess fat from the pan, then add the remaining oil and fry the onion until softened. Add the apple and cook for a further 1–2 minutes. Stir in the flour and cook for 1 minute. Add the cider and bring to the boil for 1–2 minutes. Add the stock, thyme, bay leaf and chicken.

● **3** Bring to the boil, then reduce the heat, cover and simmer for 20–25 minutes until the chicken is cooked through. Stir in the double cream and season with freshly ground black pepper.

Calories per portion 430 Kcal ● Fat per portion 34g ● Serves 4

Serve with...

Serve with creamy mashed potato and green vegetables to complete the meal.

Why not try...

You could use pork chops instead of chicken; they may need an extra 5 minutes to cook through. Replace the bay leaf with a few fresh sage leaves.

Make it at the Weekend

Chicken & Herb Savoury Loaf

Preparation time 30 minutes ● Cooking time 1 hour 10 minutes

1 small bunch flat leaf parsley

4 stems fresh tarragon

10 stems fresh chives

5 large fresh basil leaves

6 teaspoons virgin olive oil

1 shallot, chopped

250g (9oz) skinless chicken breasts

Salt and freshly ground black pepper

4 eggs

1 teaspoon dried herbes de Provence

100ml (3½fl oz) white wine

200g (7oz) flour

1 sachet easy-blend dried yeast

● **1** Preheat the oven to 180°C/350°F/Gas 4. Coarsely chop the herbs and set aside. Heat 2 teaspoons oil in a frying pan and cook the shallot for 5 minutes, stirring regularly, until soft and starting to caramelize.

● **2** Add the chicken breasts and seasoning and cook for 4–5 minutes until the chicken starts to brown. Remove from the heat. Beat together the eggs, herbes de Provence, remaining olive oil and some seasoning. Mix the flour and yeast in a bowl and stir in the egg mixture until smooth. Leave to stand for 5–10 minutes.

● **3** Dice the cooked chicken and add to the flour mixture along with the shallots and fresh herbs. Pour the mixture into a non-stick loaf tin. Bake on the bottom shelf of the oven for 10 minutes.

● **4** Turn the heat down to 160°C/325°F/Gas 3 and continue to cook for 40–45 minutes until risen and golden. Allow to cool for 10 minutes before turning out of the tin. Slice and serve warm.

Calories per portion 266 Kcal ● Fat per portion 9.4g ● Makes 6 slices

Serve with...

This makes a delicious summer lunch served with a fresh green salad.

Why not try...

If you don't have a non-stick loaf tin, line it with a strip of baking paper to make it easier to turn out.

Make it spicy...

Add a pinch or two of dried chilli flakes for some added heat.

✓ *Easy* *Spicy*

Hot Paprika Chicken with Leek Couscous

Preparation time 10 minutes ● Cooking time 35 minutes

300g carton Greek yogurt

2–3 teaspoons hot paprika

Salt and freshly ground black pepper

4 chicken pieces, thighs or breasts, skin on

225g (8oz) couscous

450ml (¾pt) hot vegetable or chicken stock

Drizzle of olive oil

4 leeks, finely chopped

Chopped fresh parsley, to garnish

Why not try...

If you have time, leave the chicken to marinate in the yogurt mixture overnight in the fridge.

- **1** Preheat the oven to 200°C/400°F/Gas 6. Mix together the yogurt and paprika in a large bowl and season with salt and pepper. Add the chicken and turn to coat.

- **2** Heat a large frying pan or griddle until hot, then add the chicken and cook until golden all over, then transfer to a roasting tin and bake for 20–25 minutes until the chicken is cooked through.

- **3** Place the couscous in a large bowl, then pour over the stock. Set aside for 10 minutes until the liquid is absorbed and the couscous is tender.

- **4** Heat the oil in a large frying pan, add the leeks and cook gently until softened but not browned. Fluff up the couscous with a fork then stir in the leeks and season with salt and freshly ground black pepper. Serve with the chicken scattered with chopped fresh parsley.

Calories per portion 490 Kcal ● Fat per portion 19g ● Serves 4

Individual Chicken Wellingtons

Preparation time 20 minutes + chilling ● Cooking time 25 minutes

2 skinless, boneless chicken breasts

75g (3oz) chicken liver pâté

250g (9oz) puff pastry, thawed if frozen

1 egg, beaten

Salt and freshly ground black pepper

● **1** Preheat the oven to 200°C/400°F/Gas 6. Trim off any fat from the chicken, then generously spread the pâté on both sides of each breast.

● **2** Roll out the pastry to 4mm (¼in) thick. Cut out 2 x 13cm (5in) squares and 2 x 15cm (6in) squares. Brush the smaller squares with egg and place a chicken breast on each. Season well.

● **3** Brush the edges of the larger squares with egg, turn over and use to cover the chicken. Pinch the edges to seal the parcels. Chill for 20–30 minutes.

● **4** Brush the top of the pastry parcels with egg and place on a baking tray. Bake for 20-25 minutes until golden brown and cooked through.

Calories per portion 771 Kcal ● Fat per portion 44.6g ● Serves 2

Serve with...

Serve the Wellingtons with baby carrots and a lightly tossed salad plus some white wine or chicken gravy.

Why not try...

This recipe can also be made with skinless duck breasts. They take longer to cook so fry them first in a little butter and oil until browned all over then add the pâté and pastry.

✓ *Easy* ❄ *Freeze it*

Hungarian Chicken

Preparation time 10 minutes ● Cooking time 30 minutes

2–3 tablespoons olive oil

500g (1lb 2oz) skinless chicken breasts, cut into strips

1 large onion, halved and sliced

1 red and 1 green pepper, deseeded and thinly sliced

2 tablespoons plain flour

2 teaspoons paprika, plus extra, to garnish

225ml (8fl oz) chicken stock

2–3 tablespoons sun-dried tomato paste

Salt and freshly ground black pepper

150ml (¼pt) soured cream

4 pickled gherkins, cut into thin strips

● **1** Heat the oil in a large lidded frying pan. Add the chicken and cook over a medium heat until lightly browned, then remove from the pan. Add the onion and peppers to the pan and cook gently until softened.

● **2** Return the chicken to the pan, then stir in the flour and paprika. Add the stock and tomato paste and bring to the boil, stirring. Reduce the heat, cover and simmer gently for 15–20 minutes until the chicken is tender.

● **3** Season with salt and pepper and serve topped with soured cream, gherkins and a dusting of paprika.

Calories per portion 355 Kcal ● Fat per portion 6g ● Serves 4

Serve with...

Cooked white rice is the ideal accompaniment to this dish. To save time, use 2 sachets of ready-cooked rice that can be quickly heated in the microwave.

Why not try...

You could make this recipe with pork fillet instead of chicken if you prefer. The cooking time will stay the same.

✓ *Easy* ❄ *Freeze it*

Chicken Curry

Preparation time 10 minutes ● Cooking time 45 minutes

2 tablespoons oil

1 large onion, finely chopped

1 clove garlic, crushed

1 teaspoon turmeric

½ teaspoon chilli powder

1½ teaspoons ground coriander

1½ teaspoons ground cumin

3 tomatoes, quartered

Salt

600g (1¼lb) cooked chicken, skinned and cut into chunks

1 teaspoon garam masala

150ml (¼pt) thick natural yogurt

Chopped fresh coriander, to garnish

Serve with...

Complete the meal with basmati rice and warm naan breads.

Make it spicy...

For an extra kick, use hot chilli powder and increase the amount to 1 teaspoon or add a finely chopped red or green chilli with the onion in step 1.

● **1** Heat the oil in a large frying pan, add the onion and garlic and fry gently for 15 minutes until softened and golden. Add the turmeric, chilli powder, ground coriander and cumin and cook for 1 minute, stirring.

● **2** Add the tomatoes and season with salt. Bring to the boil, then reduce the heat, cover and simmer for 20 minutes.

● **3** Add the chicken, garam masala and 4 tablespoons yogurt to the pan. Cover and cook gently for 10 minutes, then stir in the rest of the yogurt. Serve garnished with chopped fresh coriander.

Calories per portion 280 Kcal ● Fat per portion 13g ● Serves 4

✓ *Easy* ❄ *Freeze it*

Chicken & Parsnip Stew

Preparation time 15 minutes ● Cooking time 2 hours

1 tablespoon olive oil
1 whole chicken, jointed (ask your butcher to do this) or use 4 chicken pieces (legs and thighs)
Pinch freshly grated nutmeg
Zest of 1 small orange
Salt and freshly ground black pepper
1 onion, roughly chopped
Handful fresh thyme sprigs
4 medium parsnips, roughly chopped
2 red apples, sliced
200g (7oz) button or chestnut mushrooms
600ml (1pt) hot chicken stock

● **1** Preheat the oven to 190°C/375°F/Gas 5. Heat the oil in a large ovenproof casserole and fry the chicken pieces until golden brown on all sides. Turn off the heat, then sprinkle with nutmeg and orange zest. Season.

● **2** Add the onion, thyme, parsnips, apples and mushrooms to the casserole and pack in tightly. Pour over the hot stock and season. Bake for 2 hours until the chicken is cooked and the parsnips are soft. You can turn the heat down and continue cooking on low till you are ready to eat.

Calories per portion 313 Kcal ● Fat per portion 8g ● Serves 4

Serve with...

Fresh crusty bread is all you need to complete this hearty meal.

Why not try...

Once the casserole is cooked you can turn the heat down low and keep it warm until you are ready to serve.

Make it at the Weekend

Chicken, Broccoli & Spinach Filo Pie

Preparation time 30 minutes ● Cooking time 45 minutes

2 skinless chicken breasts

2 tablespoons olive oil

Salt and freshly ground black pepper

1 head broccoli, cut into florets

200g (7oz) chestnut mushrooms, sliced

Pinch dried chilli flakes

Zest of 1 lemon

½ x 200g bag spinach

1 egg, lightly beaten

25g (1oz) butter, melted, for glazing

10 sheets filo pastry

Serve with...

A simple green salad goes well with this pie or serve with jacket potatoes for a heartier meal.

Make it spicy...

For an extra spicy kick, brush the chicken with chilli oil before roasting and add a sliced red chilli to the mushrooms in step 2.

● **1** Preheat the oven to 180°C/350°F/Gas 4. Place the chicken in a roasting tin, drizzle with half the oil and season with salt and pepper. Roast for 20 minutes until the chicken is cooked through. Set aside. Cook the broccoli in a large pan of boiling, salted water until tender. Drain and set aside.

● **2** Heat the remaining oil in a large frying pan and cook the mushrooms until soft and they release their juices. Add the chilli flakes, lemon zest and spinach and stir until wilted. Season well. Allow to cool slightly, then stir in the egg. Slice the chicken and add to the spinach mixture with the broccoli.

● **3** Brush a pie dish with a little melted butter. Lay 4 sheets of filo in the base to cover. Spoon in half the chicken mixture, then cover with 2 more filo sheets and top with the remaining chicken. Pull the sides of the pastry in, then lay the remaining sheets on top and tuck down the sides neatly.

● 4 Brush the pastry evenly with melted butter. Mark lightly into squares with a serrated knife, then bake for 15–20 minutes until golden.

Calories per portion 311 Kcal ● Fat per portion 15g ● Serves 4

✓ *Easy*

Stuffed Chicken with Goats' Cheese

Preparation time 15 minutes ● Cooking time 40 minutes

150g tub soft goats' cheese
Bunch fresh thyme, chopped, few sprigs reserved
200g can pitted green olives, drained, half chopped
Salt and freshly ground black pepper
4 chicken breast or thigh fillets, skin on
450g (1lb) baby new potatoes, halved
Olive oil, to drizzle

- **1** Preheat the oven to 200°C/400°F/Gas 6. In a small bowl, mix the goats' cheese with 2 tablespoons chopped thyme, the chopped olives and plenty of salt and pepper. Peel back part of chicken skin to make an opening and stuff the cheese mixture under the skin.

- **2** Place the chicken in a roasting dish. Add the potatoes and drizzle with a little olive oil until well coated. Season with salt and pepper and a handful of thyme sprigs. Roast for 35–40 minutes until the chicken is golden, crispy and cooked through. Serve with the remaining olives scattered over.

Calories per portion 560 Kcal ● Fat per portion 30g ● Serves 4

Why not try...

Instead of making your own stuffing, use a tub of soft cheese flavoured with garlic and herbs.

Quick ✓ Easy

Warm Coronation Chicken Salad

Preparation time 10 minutes ● Cooking time 20 minutes

150g carton plain natural yogurt

1 tablespoon hot curry paste

1 tablespoon apricot jam

Zest and juice of ½ lime

4 skinless, boneless chicken breasts

1 mango, peeled and cut into chunks

4 spring onions, thinly sliced

150g bag salad leaves

2 tablespoons roughly chopped fresh coriander

● **1** In a large bowl, mix together the yogurt, curry paste and jam. Place 2 tablespoons in another bowl, add the lime zest and juice and set aside. Add the chicken to the remaining yogurt mixture and mix well to coat.

● **2** Preheat the grill to high. Place the chicken on a grill rack and cook for 7–8 minutes on each side, until cooked through. Leave to rest for 5 minutes, then cut into bite-size pieces.

● **3** Meanwhile, in a large bowl, mix the mango with the spring onions and salad leaves. Pour over the yogurt and lime dressing and toss to mix. Add the chicken and coriander to the salad and serve immediately.

Calories per portion 251 Kcal ● Fat per portion 8g ● Serves 4

Serve with...

Serve this flavour-packed salad with warm pitta breads.

Why not try...

If you have time, marinate the chicken breasts in the yogurt mixture for about an hour. This makes them extra succulent and tasty.

Make it at the Weekend

Pot Roast Minty Chicken

Preparation time 20 minutes ● Cooking time 1½ hours

- Salt and freshly ground black pepper
- 1.3–1.8kg (3–4lb) chicken
- 2 tablespoons olive oil
- 25g (1oz) butter, plus 50g (2oz) cold butter, cubed
- 1 onion, roughly chopped
- 2 celery sticks, chopped
- 1 garlic clove
- 10 fresh mint leaves, 5 shredded
- 850ml (1½pts) chicken stock or water
- 225g (8oz) frozen peas
- 225g (8oz) button mushrooms, quartered
- 150ml (¼pt) double cream

● **Step 1** Season the chicken. Heat the oil and half the butter in a frying pan and brown the chicken on all sides until golden. Transfer to a casserole dish.

● **2** Preheat the oven to 200°C/400°F/Gas 6. Fry the onion, celery, garlic clove and whole mint leaves for 4–5 minutes. Add to the chicken in the dish.

● **3** Warm the stock and pour over the chicken and vegetables in the pot. Cover and roast for 1 hour, basting occasionally, until cooked. Remove the chicken from the dish and leave to rest, loosely covered in foil.

● **Step 4** Cook the peas in boiling salted water until tender. Season the mushrooms and fry in the remaining 15g (½oz) butter until tender.

● **Step 5** Strain the chicken cooking liquid into a pan and boil rapidly for 10 minutes until reduced by half. Add the cream and simmer for 3–4 minutes.

● **6** Carve the chicken. Add the mushrooms and peas to the sauce and heat through. Stir in the cold butter, season, add the shredded mint and serve.

Calories per portion 582 Kcal ● Fat per portion 48.2g ● Serves 6

Step 1 *Cook the chicken in oil and butter in a frying pan until golden all over then transfer to a casserole dish.*

Step 4 *Fry the quartered button mushrooms in a frying pan, stirring regularly, until golden and tender.*

Step 5 *Add the double cream to the reduced cooking liquid and simmer, stirring, for 3-4 minutes.*

✓ *Easy* *Spicy*

Eastern Spicy Chicken

Preparation time 10 minutes ● Cooking time 50 minutes

2–3 tablespoons olive oil

4 chicken portions

2 onions, chopped

4 garlic cloves, chopped

5cm (2in) piece fresh ginger, sliced

1 red chilli, finely sliced

300ml (½pt) vegetable stock

Salt and freshly ground black pepper

Fresh chopped coriander, to garnish

● **1** Heat 2 tablespoons oil in a large frying pan and brown the chicken portions on both sides. Transfer to a plate. Add the onions to the pan and fry until softened, then add the garlic, ginger and chilli. Cook for a further 2 minutes, then return the chicken to the pan.

● **2** Pour in the stock and bring to the boil. Reduce the heat, cover and simmer for 30 minutes until the chicken is cooked through. Taste the sauce and season if needed. Sprinkle with coriander and serve.

Calories per portion 508 Kcal ● Fat per portion 35.2g ● Serves 4

Serve with...

Serve the chicken on a bed of egg noodles tossed with a little soy sauce.

Why not try...

The chicken also tastes good served cold as part of a picnic or buffet.

✓ *Easy* Ⓝ *Contains Nuts*

Chicken & Broad Beans with Pesto

Preparation time 10 minutes ● Cooking time 35 minutes

1 tablespoon olive oil

2 chicken breasts, about 175g (6oz) each

250g (9oz) broad beans, thawed if frozen

75g (3oz) mixed pitted olives, halved

1 large orange, peeled, segmented and cut into small pieces

For the dressing

25g (1oz) shelled walnuts

2 tablespoons olive oil

½ bunch fresh tarragon

1 bunch fresh flat-leaf parsley

1 teaspoon cider or white wine vinegar

Salt and freshly ground black pepper

● **1** Preheat the oven to 200°C/400°F/Gas 6. Heat the oil in a large frying pan and fry the chicken until golden all over. Transfer to an ovenproof dish, cover with foil and roast for 20–30 minutes until cooked through. Remove from the oven and leave to cool, then slice and set aside.

● **2** Cook the broad beans in a pan of boiling, salted water for 3 minutes, then drain and refresh under cold water running water.

● **3** To make the dressing, blitz the walnuts in a food processor until finely chopped, then add the oil, tarragon, half the parsley, the vinegar and 2 tablespoons water. Blitz again until smooth, then season.

● **4** Arrange the chicken in a large serving dish, then add the beans, olives, orange and remaining parsley, torn into pieces. Spoon over the walnut pesto dressing just before serving.

Calories per portion 274 Kcal ● Fat per portion 17g ● Serves 4

Serve with...

Top the salad with slices of toasted French stick or other rustic bread.

Why not try...

If you have time, you can peel the broad beans by slipping them out of their skins after cooking in step 2.

✓ *Easy*

Warm Chicken & Potato Salad

Preparation time 10 minutes ● Cooking time 30 minutes

1kg (2lb 4oz) baby new potatoes

1 garlic clove, peeled and left whole

1 orange, skin left on, sliced into rings

2 tablespoons olive oil

Salt and freshly ground black pepper

4 ready-cooked chargrilled chicken breasts, sliced

125g (4oz) ready-to-eat dried apricots, chopped

Bunch fresh flat-leaf parsley, chopped

Zest and juice of 1 orange

● **1** Preheat the oven to 220°C/425°F/Gas 7. Put the potatoes, garlic and orange slices in a roasting tin and drizzle with half the oil. Shake to coat the potatoes with the oil and season. Roast for 30 minutes until the potatoes are golden and crisp. Gently crush the potatoes with a fork.

● **2** Transfer the potatoes and orange slices to a large bowl, add the chicken, apricots and parsley and stir to combine.

● **3** For the dressing, place the remaining oil in a jug and squeeze in the roasted garlic pulp from its skin. Whisk in the orange zest and juice and season. Drizzle over the warm potatoes and serve.

Calories per portion 330 Kcal ● Fat per portion 19g ● Serves 4

Why not try...

This dish is also delicious made with smoked duck instead of chicken.

Make it at the Weekend ❄ Freeze it

Chicken & Apple Crumble

Preparation time 20 minutes ● Cooking time 45 minutes

700g (1½lbs) skinless chicken breasts, cut into 1cm (½in) pieces
1 onion, chopped
1 garlic clove, crushed
Salt and freshly ground black pepper
1 tablespoon plain flour
2 teaspoons vegetable oil
1 tablespoon wholegrain mustard
300ml (½pt) chicken stock
200ml (7fl oz) cider
200g (7oz) Bramley apples, cored and cubed
3 teaspoons chopped fresh thyme

For the crumble

150g (5oz) plain flour
1 teaspoon mustard powder
50g (2oz) butter, cubed
50g (2oz) strong Cheddar, grated

Serve with...

A selection of seasonal vegetables is the ideal accompaniment to this autumnal dish. Try roasted butternut squash or some lightly fried mixed mushrooms.

- **1** Preheat the oven to 200°C/400°F/Gas 6. Heat the oil in a large frying pan over a medium heat and fry the chicken for 7–10 minutes until golden brown. Add the onion, garlic, seasoning and 2 teaspoons thyme. Stir in the flour and cook for 1 minute, stirring continuously.
- **2** Add the wholegrain mustard, chicken stock and cider and simmer for 10 minutes until the liquid is reduced and thickened. (If it still seems too runny, tip away some of the liquid.)
- **3** Meanwhile make the crumble topping. Sift the flour, mustard powder and a pinch of salt into a mixing bowl. Rub in the butter and cheese with your fingers until the mixture resembles large crumbs. Add the remaining thyme.
- **4** In a large ovenproof dish, combine the chicken mixture and apples. Cover with a thick layer of crumble topping. Bake for 25 minutes until golden.

Calories per portion 542 Kcal ● Fat per portion 20.3g ● Serves 4

Super Quick ✓✓ Extra Easy

Mustard Chicken

Preparation time 5 minutes ● Cooking time 10 minutes

4 skinless, boneless chicken breasts, cut into chunks
Salt and freshly ground black pepper
1 tablespoon olive oil
1 teaspoon paprika
2 tablespoons wholegrain mustard
150ml (¼pt) white wine
200ml tub crème fraîche

- **1** Season the chicken with salt and freshly ground black pepper. Heat the oil in a pan and fry the chicken for 5 minutes until browned all over.
- **2** Add the paprika, mustard and white wine and allow to bubble for 2–3 minutes until the chicken is cooked through. Stir in the crème fraiche, season and serve immediately.

Calories per portion 420 Kcal ● Fat per portion 30g ● Serves 4

Serve with...

This flavoursome dish goes beautifully with steamed leeks.

Why not try...

You could use pork fillet or lean beef steaks for this recipe instead of chicken. The cooking time will be the same.

Make it at the Weekend

Japanese Fried Chicken

Preparation time 20 minutes + marinating ● Cooking time 10 minutes

8–10 skinless, boneless chicken thighs or 600g (1lb 6oz) chicken breasts, cut into 2.5cm (1in) cubes

2.5cm (1in) piece fresh ginger, finely grated

3 tablespoons Mirin (rice wine, similar to sake)

3 tablespoons dark soy sauce

125g (4oz) cornflour

¼ teaspoon coarse rock salt

Vegetable oil, for deep frying

Cucumber strips, to garnish

● **1** Place the chicken in a large flat dish and prick all over with a skewer. Squeeze the fresh ginger over a bowl until you get about 2 teaspoons juice. (Grate some more ginger if you don't get enough.) Add the Mirin and soy sauce and mix well. Pour over the chicken and stir to coat. Cover and marinate for 20 minutes in the fridge.

● **2** In a separate dish mix the cornflour and salt. Roll each chicken piece in the flour mixture until lightly coated.

● **3** Heat about 5cm (2in) oil in the deep pan over a medium heat until it bubbles gently when a cube of bread is dropped in. (Do no overheat or allow to smoke.) Add a few pieces of chicken at a time and cook for 4 minutes, turning regularly, until crisp and golden brown all over. Drain on kitchen paper. Garnish with cucumber and serve hot.

Calories per portion 332 Kcal ● Fat per portion 15.9g ● Serves 6

Serve with...

Boiled or steamed jasmine rice goes well with this dish.

Make it spicy...

Add a sliced red chilli to the marinade in step 1.

Super Quick ✓ *Easy* *Contains Nuts*

Pesto Pasta with Chicken

Preparation time 5 minutes ● Cooking time 10 minutes

500g pack tagliatelle

1½ tablespoons olive oil

250g pack mushrooms, sliced

2 garlic cloves, finely chopped

600g (1¼lb) cooked chicken, cut into even-sized pieces

Salt and freshly ground black pepper

4 tablespoons green pesto

2 tablespoons finely chopped fresh tarragon

● **1** Cook the pasta in a pan of boiling salted water according to the packet instructions. Meanwhile, heat the olive oil in a frying pan and fry the mushrooms for 2–3 minutes, then add the garlic and chicken, season with salt and freshly ground black pepper and cook until heated through.

● **2** Drain the pasta, return to the pan and stir in the pesto. Add the tarragon to the chicken mixture and add to the pasta. Toss to mix and serve.

Calories per portion 520 Kcal ● Fat per portion 15g ● Serves 6

Serve with...

This dish tastes great on its own but you could add some grated Parmesan and warm garlic bread if you like.

Why not try...

We've used a classic green pesto made with basil but there are plenty of other varieties in the supermarkets you could try. Rocket pesto or aubergine pesto would work well.

Make it at the Weekend

Chicken Burrito

Preparation time 30 minutes ● Cooking time 25 minutes

225g (8oz) plain flour

Salt

1 tablespoon lard or vegetable fat

125ml (4fl oz) warm water

3 cooked chicken breasts, shredded

½ crisp lettuce, finely shredded

200g (7oz) fresh tomato salsa

Serve with...

For a Mexican feast, serve with rice, refried beans and guacamole.

Why not try...

To save time, use ready-made flour tortillas and heat through according to the packet instructions before filling.

● **Step 1** Sift the flour and salt into a large bowl. Rub in the lard or vegetable fat with your fingertips until the mixture resembles coarse breadcrumbs.

● **2** Gradually add 125ml (4fl oz) warm water and mix to a soft dough. Knead lightly, form into a ball, cover with a cloth and leave to rest for 15 minutes.

● **3** Divide the dough into 12 portions and shape into balls. Roll out each ball of dough on a lightly floured board to a 15cm (6in) circle.

● **Step 4** Heat a griddle or non-stick frying pan over a medium heat. Cook the tortillas one at a time, for 1½–2 minutes each side until lightly browned.

● **Step 5** Place 1 tablespoon chicken in the centre of a tortilla with a little lettuce and salsa. Fold in 2 sides to create a roll. Fold in the ends to make a parcel. Place, flap side down, on a plate. Serve with the remaining salsa.

Calories per portion 90 Kcal ● Fat per portion 1g ● Makes 12

Step 1 *Lightly rub the fat into the flour with your fingertips until the mixture resembles coarse breadcrumbs.*

Step 4 *Cook the tortillas on a hot griddle or non-stick frying pan until lightly browned on both sides.*

Step 5 *Fold in two sides of the tortilla to make a roll then fold in the ends to enclose the filling in a parcel.*

✓ *Easy* ❄ *Freeze it*

Orange & Tomato Chicken

Preparation time 10 minutes ● Cooking time 1¼ hours

2 tablespoons olive oil

4 chicken legs or 4–8 chicken thighs, depending on size

1 onion, sliced

2 teaspoons paprika

4 tomatoes, quartered

1 orange, halved and sliced

3 medium potatoes, peeled and cut into wedges

100ml (3½fl oz) chicken stock or water

2 tablespoons pitted green olives, optional

● **1** Preheat the oven to 180C/350F/Gas 4. Heat the oil in a large, lidded casserole and brown the chicken all over. Remove from the dish and set aside. Add the onion and cook gently, stirring regularly, until softened.

● **2** Stir in the paprika then add all the remaining ingredients, except the olives and stir together. Sit the chicken on top of the vegetables, then cover and cook for 1–1¼ hours until the potatoes are tender and the chicken is cooked through. Stir in the olives just before serving.

Calories per portion 316 Kcal ● Fat per portion 9g ● Serves 4

Serve with...

A loaf of crusty bread and some steamed broccoli or mangetout go well with this casserole.

Why not try...

Replace half the stock or water with red wine for a richer flavour.

✓ Easy ❄ *Freeze it*

Slow-cooked Chicken

Preparation time 5 minutes ● Cooking time 40 minutes

Small knob butter

1 tablespoon olive oil

4 large or 8 small chicken thighs

4 garlic cloves

Few sprigs fresh thyme

Salt and freshly ground black pepper

250ml (9fl oz) white wine

250ml (9fl oz) chicken stock

● **1** Heat the butter and oil in a casserole dish. Brown the chicken, skin-side down, for 5 minutes. Flatten the garlic with the flat side of a knife and remove the skin. Turn the chicken over and add the garlic, thyme and seasoning to dish. Cover and cook gently for 30 minutes.

● **2** Remove the chicken from the dish and drain off as much fat as possible while keeping chicken juices. Return the dish to the heat and whisk in the wine and stock. Bubble for 3–4 minutes. Pour over the chicken and serve.

Calories per portion 256 Kcal ● Fat per portion 9g ● Serves 4

Serve with...

This tender chicken dish goes well with creamy mash or fluffy baked potatoes and seasonal vegetables.

Why not try...

You could use chicken breasts instead of thighs if you prefer. Reduce the cooking time by about 5–10 minutes.

✓ *Easy*

Chicken Thighs with Sweet Potato

Preparation time 15 minutes plus marinating ● Cooking time 30 minutes

8 chicken thighs, skin on

1 tablespoon smooth mustard

1 tablespoon clear honey

Generous splash soy sauce

Salt and freshly ground black pepper

Splash olive oil

4 sweet potatoes, peeled and roughly chopped

2 red peppers, peeled and roughly chopped

● **1** Preheat the oven to 200°C/400°F/Gas 6. Mix together the chicken, mustard, honey and soy sauce in a bowl. Stir well and season. Leave to marinate for 1 hour, if you have the time, or cook straight away.

● **2** In a large frying pan, heat the oil and cook the chicken, skin side down, in two batches, until starting to brown. Turn over and cook for 2 minutes.

● **3** Transfer the chicken to a roasting tin and add the potatoes and peppers. Roast for 20 minutes until golden and tender and the chicken is cooked.

Calories per portion 511 Kcal ● Fat per portion 17g ● Serves 4

Serve with...

Simply serve this tasty roast with some baby spinach leaves.

Make it spicy...

Replace the honey and mustard with sweet chilli sauce.

✓ Easy *Spicy*

Cajun Chicken with Corn Relish

Preparation time 10 minutes plus 15 minutes chilling ● Cooking time 30 minutes

2–3 teaspoons Cajun seasoning

6 chicken breasts, slashed

Zest and juice of 1 lime

2 tablespoons olive oil

2 red peppers, deseeded and finely chopped

1 red chilli, deseeded and finely chopped

198g can sweetcorn, drained

400g can chopped tomatoes

1 tablespoon red wine vinegar

½ teaspoon caster sugar

Salt and freshly ground black pepper

● **1** Rub the Cajun seasoning over the chicken, add the lime zest, juice and half the oil. Cover and chill in the fridge for 15 minutes.

● **2** Heat the remaining oil in a pan and fry the peppers and chilli until tender. Add the sweetcorn, tomatoes, red wine vinegar, sugar, salt and pepper. Bring to the boil and simmer for 3–5 minutes.

● **3** Cook the chicken breasts on a hot barbecue or grill for 15–20 minutes, basting occasionally with the remaining marinade, until cooked through and the juices run clear when the chicken is pierced with a knife. Serve with warm or cold sweetcorn relish.

Calories per portion 270 Kcal ● Fat per portion 11g ● Serves 6

Serve with...

This recipe goes really well with sweet potatoes and chilli butter, and a simple green salad.

Quick ✓ *Easy*

Chicken Tikka with Lime & Mint

Preparation time 10 minutes ● Cooking time 15 minutes

150g tub 0% fat Greek yogurt
1 teaspoon mild, medium or hot curry powder
Juice of 1 lime
Handful fresh mint leaves, roughly chopped
4 skinless boneless chicken breasts

For the salad
200g bag baby spinach leaves
Handful fresh mint, roughly chopped
1 teaspoon extra-virgin olive oil
Juice of ½ lime
Salt
Lime wedges and coriander, to garnish

● **1** Mix together the yogurt, curry powder, lime juice and fresh mint in a bowl until combined. Add the chicken breasts and turn until coated.

● **2** Preheat the grill to high. Cook the chicken on a grill rack for 6 minutes on each side until cooked through and lightly browned.

● **3** Meanwhile, prepare the salad. Tip the spinach and mint leaves onto a platter or serving dish. Drizzle with oil and lime juice, then toss together with a sprinkling of salt. Roughly slice the chicken and arrange on top. Serve with lime wedges and coriander leaves.

Calories per portion 308 Kcal ● Fat per portion 10g ● Serves 4

Why not try...
If you have time, put the chicken and marinade in a plastic food bag at the end of step 1 and marinate in the fridge for 2 hours or overnight.

✓ *Easy* ❄ *Freeze it* Ⓝ *Contains Nuts*

Thai Green Chicken Curry

Preparation time 10 minutes ● Cooking time 35 minutes

2 teaspoons peanut or vegetable oil

2 tablespoons Thai green curry paste

750g (1lb 10oz) skinless chicken breast or thigh fillets, cubed

1 large red chilli, sliced

6 spring onions, sliced

400g can coconut milk

250ml (9fl oz) chicken stock

150g (5oz) green beans, trimmed

1 tablespoon fish sauce

Juice of ½ lime

3 tablespoons roughly chopped fresh coriander

● **Step 1** Heat the oil in a large pan over a medium heat. Add the curry paste and stir for 1–2 minutes. Add the chicken, chilli and spring onions and cook for 5 minutes until lightly browned.

● **Step 2** Stir in the coconut milk and chicken stock, bring to the boil, then cover and simmer over a medium heat for 15 minutes.

● **Step 3** Add the green beans and cook, uncovered, for 8–10 minutes until the beans are tender. Stir in the fish sauce, lime juice and coriander. Serve.

Calories per portion 268 Kcal ● Fat per portion 6g ● Serves 4

Step 1 *Add the chicken, chilli and spring onions and cook for 5 minutes, stirring regularly, until lightly browned.*

Step 2 *Pour in the coconut milk and chicken stock, stir well and bring to the boil over a medium heat.*

Step 3 *Add the fish sauce, lime juice and coriander to the curry just before serving to keep the flavours fresh.*

Perfect Roast Chicken

Preparation time 20 minutes ● Cooking time 2 hours

2kg (4½lb) chicken

1 lemon

1 tablespoon olive oil

1 tablespoon plain flour

600ml (1pt) hot chicken stock

For the stuffing

1 large onion, chopped

1 tablespoon olive oil

25g (1oz) butter

225g (8oz) fresh breadcrumbs

Zest of 1 lemon

2 tablespoons each chopped fresh parsley and thyme

Salt and freshly ground black pepper

● **1** Preheat the oven to 200C/400F/Gas 6. To make the stuffing, cook the onion in the oil for 5 minutes until softened. Mix with the remaining ingredients and season.

● **2** Wipe the chicken inside and out with kitchen paper. Season the cavity and insert half the lemon. With bird breast-side down, season the neck end and spoon in the stuffing.

● **3** Slice the remaining lemon and carefully insert under the skin over the chicken breast. Cover the breast with oil. Place the chicken, breast side down, on a rack in a roasting tin.

● **4** Roast the chicken for 20 minutes per 450g (1lb), plus 20 minutes, basting frequently. After 15–20 minutes, turn breast-side up and continue cooking.

● **5** Remove the chicken from the tin and drain off the excess fat. Sprinkle in the flour and stir well over a medium heat. Slowly add the stock and bring to the boil. Simmer for 2 minutes. Serve with the chicken and stuffing.

Calories per portion 465 Kcal ● Fat per portion 32g ● Serves 6

Serve with...

Roast potatoes, steamed broccoli and broad beans make an ideal accompaniment to this dish.

Why not try...

If you prefer a thicker gravy, boil for a further 5 minutes before serving.

❄ *Freeze it* Ⓝ *Contains Nuts*

Chicken & Chestnut Crumble

Preparation time 10 minutes ● Cooking time 45 minutes

3 skinless, boneless chicken breasts

450ml (¾pt) chicken stock

2 leeks, sliced

40g (1½oz) butter

½ teaspoon plain flour

125g (4oz) canned or vacuum-packed chestnuts, roughly chopped

1 tablespoon chopped fresh sage

2 dessert apples, sliced

For the crumble

100g (3½oz) plain flour

50g (2oz) cold butter, cubed

50g (2oz) Gruyère, grated

¼ teaspoon cayenne pepper

❄ *Why not try...*

To freeze the crumble, assemble as directed but do not bake. Allow to cool then wrap in freezer film and foil. Freeze for up to 3 months. Allow to thaw before baking.

● **1** Preheat the oven to 200°C/400°F/Gas 6. Heat the stock in a pan until just simmering. Add the chicken and poach gently for 7 minutes until cooked through. Remove with a slotted spoon, then cool and slice. Return the stock to the boil, add the leeks and cook for 2 minutes. Drain, reserving the stock.

● **2** In a clean pan, melt the butter, then stir in the flour and cook, stirring, for 1 minute. Gradually add the reserved stock. Cook for 2 minutes, whisking.

● **3** Place the chicken, leeks, chestnuts, sage and apples in an ovenproof casserole dish and toss gently to mix. Pour over the sauce.

● **4** In a food processor, briefly whizz the flour and butter until the mixture resembles breadcrumbs. Tip into a bowl, add the cheese and cayenne and season with salt. Sprinkle evenly over the chicken mixture and bake for 30 minutes until browned and bubbling.

Calories per portion 520 Kcal ● Fat per portion 26g ● Serves 4

Make it at the Weekend ✓ *Easy*

Roast Chicken with Garlic

Preparation time 20 minutes ● Cooking time 1¾ hours

15g (½oz) butter

2 teaspoons olive oil

1 large chicken

4 garlic bulbs, separated into cloves

1 onion, chopped

5–6 shallots, chopped

2–3 sprigs fresh rosemary

2–3 bay leaves

Salt and freshly ground black pepper

275ml (10fl oz) white wine

● **1** Preheat the oven to 200°C/400°F/Gas 6. Melt the butter and oil in a flameproof casserole dish. Keeping the heat high, add the chicken and fry, turning regularly, until browned on all sides. This will take 10–15 minutes.

● **2** Transfer the chicken to a plate and add the garlic cloves, onion and shallots to the dish. Put the chicken on top and sprinkle over the rosemary, bay leaves and seasoning. Pour in the wine and bring to a gentle simmer.

● **3** Cover with a lid and roast in the oven for 1 hour 15 minutes. Remove the lid and cook for a further 10 minutes to brown the chicken. Check the chicken is cooked thoroughly by pricking the thickest part of the meat with a skewer – the juices should run clear.

● **4** Allow to stand for 10 minutes, then carve the chicken and serve with the juices from the dish and the garlic, onions and shallots.

● Calories per portion 395 Kcal ● Fat per portion 21.6g ● Serves 6

Serve with...

Serve the chicken with a selection of vegetables such as peas, carrots and broccoli. The roasted garlic can also be eaten. Simply squash the cloves with a knife to reveal the soft sweet flesh and eat with the chicken or spread on fresh crusty bread.

Quick ✓ Easy N Contains Nuts

Chicken Satay

Preparation time 10 minutes ● Cooking time 20 minutes

2 skinless, boneless chicken breasts or thighs, cut into strips
400g can coconut milk
2 tablespoons crunchy peanut butter
Salt

● **1** Preheat the grill to high and line a grill rack with foil. Thread the chicken strips onto skewers in a zigzag. Set aside. Bring the coconut milk to the boil in a pan, then simmer gently for 5 minutes until slightly thickened.

● **2** Stir in the peanut butter and cook for 2–3 minutes, stirring, until smooth and combined. Season with salt. Divide the sauce between 2 bowls.

● **3** Use one bowl of sauce to cover each chicken skewer then grill for 5–8 minutes each side until the chicken is cooked through. Serve with the remaining bowl of peanut sauce.

Calories per portion 608 Kcal ● Fat per portion 43g ● Serves 2

Serve with...

These kebabs make a great snack on their own or serve on a bed of rice for a more filling meal.

Why not try...

You can use metal or wooden skewers for this dish. If using wooden skewers, soak them in cold water for 30 minutes first to stop them from burning. If you don't have skewers, just grill the chicken strips on a grill rack, turning regularly with tongs until cooked through.

Make it spicy...

To heat things up, add chilli sauce or Thai red curry paste to the simmering coconut milk.

✓ *Easy*

Chicken & Vegetable Kebabs

Preparation time 20 minutes, plus chilling ● Cooking time 15 minutes

400g packet casserole vegetables, peeled and cut into small chunks
Salt
6 tablespoons tapenade (black olive paste)
4 sprigs fresh rosemary
8 tablespoons olive oil
4 skinless, boneless chicken breasts, cut into 2.5cm (1in) cubes

● **1** Parboil the vegetables (except the onion) in a pan of boiling salted water, for 5 minutes, then drain.

● **2** In a large bowl, mix together the tapenade, rosemary and 6 tablespoons oil. Add the chicken, vegetables and onion and stir to coat. Cover and chill in the fridge for at least 30 minutes.

● **3** Preheat the grill to high. Thread the chicken and vegetables onto metal skewers. Grill on a rack for 10 minutes, turning once, until browned and the chicken is cooked through. Drizzle with the remaining oil to serve.

Calories per portion 430 Kcal ● Fat per portion 31g ● Serves 4

Serve with...

The kebabs make a great meal on their own or you could serve with some fresh crusty bread or sautéed potatoes.

Why not try...

You could make these kebabs with cubes of lean lamb instead of chicken. Grill for 8–10 minutes until just cooked through.

Make it at the Weekend *Freeze it*

Chicken & Sausage Cobbler

Preparation time 20 minutes ● Cooking time 1¾ hours

1 tablespoon olive oil

2 onions, roughly chopped

6 sausages, skins removed

375ml (14fl oz) red wine

4 chicken breasts, chopped

2 garlic cloves, roughly chopped

5 carrots, roughly chopped

600ml (1pt) hot vegetable stock

200g (7oz) self-raising flour

Salt

50g (2oz) butter

Handful fresh parsley, finely chopped, plus extra to serve

Splash of milk

1 egg, beaten

Serve with...

This cobbler is a filling meal on its own but you could serve with some steamed cabbage or spinach if you like.

Why not try...

If you don't want to add the scone topping, simply simmer the casserole for 1½ hours in step 2.

● **1** In a large flameproof casserole dish, heat the oil and fry the onions for 5 minutes. Add the sausage meat and cook until browned all over. Pour in 125ml (4fl oz) red wine and simmer until the wine evaporates.

● **2** Increase the heat a little and add the chicken. Cook until sealed all over. Add the garlic and remaining wine and simmer until the wine evaporates. Stir in the carrots and pour over the stock. Bring to the boil, reduce the heat and simmer gently for 1 hour.

● **3** Preheat the oven to 190°C/375°F/Gas 5. Place the flour and a pinch of salt in a large bowl. Rub in the butter with your fingertips until the mixture resembles breadcrumbs. Stir in the parsley. Add a few drops of milk and mix to a dough. Shape into a ball, wrap in cling film and chill for 20 minutes.

● **4** Roll out the dough on a floured board and cut out 14 rounds with a 4cm (1½in) round cutter. Place around the edge of the casserole and brush the scones with egg. Bake for 20–30 minutes until golden. Scatter with parsley.

Calories per portion 574 Kcal ● Fat per portion 28g ● Serves 6

Spicy

Spinach-stuffed Chicken

Preparation time 20 minutes ● Cooking time 40 minutes

250g (9oz) spinach leaves

1 onion, finely chopped

2 garlic cloves, finely chopped

1 red chilli, finely chopped

2 tablespoons chopped fresh parsley

2 tablespoons double cream

Salt and freshly ground black pepper

4 chicken breasts, skin on

2 tablespoons olive oil, plus extra, to serve

Balsamic vinegar, to drizzle

● **1** Preheat the oven to 190C/375F/Gas 5. Place the spinach in a large pan with 2 tablespoon water. Cover and cook gently until wilted. Drain well, pressing out as much water as you can.

● **2** Place the spinach in a bowl with the onion, garlic, chilli, parsley, cream and seasoning. Mix well until evenly combined.

● **3** Cut a slit down the side of each chicken breast to form a pocket. Spoon in the spinach mixture, pressing in well then secure with cocktail sticks. Place in a roasting tin and drizzle with the oil.

● **4** Roast for 30–35 minutes until the chicken is cooked through and golden. Slice and serve hot drizzled with a little oil and balsamic vinegar.

Calories per portion 371 Kcal ● Fat per portion 19.6g ● Serves 4

Serve with...

Serve the stuffed chicken on a bed of rice or pasta.

Why not try...

If you prefer a milder dish, omit the chilli and add a grating of nutmeg instead.

Quick ✓✓ Extra Easy

Sticky Chicken Bites

Preparation time 5 minutes plus marinating ● Cooking time 5 minutes

4 skinless, boneless chicken breasts, cut into bite-sized pieces
2 garlic cloves, crushed
25cm (1in) piece fresh ginger, peeled and grated
2 tablespoons soy sauce
2 tablespoons ketchup
1 tablespoon sweet chilli sauce
1 tablespoon sunflower oil
Sweet chilli sauce or hoisin sauce, to serve

- **1** In a bowl, mix together the garlic, ginger, soy sauce, ketchup, chilli sauce and oil. Add the chicken, mix well and marinate for at least 15 minutes.
- **2** Heat a frying pan until hot then add the chicken. Cook over a medium heat, stirring continuously, for 5 minutes until the chicken is cooked through. Serve with sweet chilli sauce or hoisin sauce for dipping.

Calories per portion 218 Kcal ● Fat per portion 9g ● Serves 4

Serve with...

Serve the chicken bites with boiled or steamed rice tossed with chopped fresh coriander.

Make it spicy...

For a spicy kick, add a chopped red chilli to the marinade.

Weights, measures & temperatures

TEMPERATURE

°C	°F	Gas	°C	°F	Gas
110	225	¼	190	375	5
120/130	250	½	200	400	6
140	275	1	220	425	7
150	300	2	230	450	8
160/170	325	3	240	475	9
180	350	4			

LIQUIDS

Metric	Imperial	Metric	Imperial
5ml	1 tsp	200ml	7fl oz
15ml	1 tbsp	250ml	9fl oz
25ml	1fl oz	300ml	½ pint
50ml	2fl oz	500ml	18fl oz
100ml	3½fl oz	600ml	1 pint
125ml	4fl oz	900ml	1½ pints
150ml	5fl oz/¼ pint	1 litre	1¾ pints
175ml	6fl oz		

ABOUT THE RECIPES

Recipes that are suitable for freezing are indicated at the top of the recipe. For further guidance, see below and consult your freezer manufacturer's guidelines.

MEASURES

Metric	Imperial	Metric	Imperial
5mm	¼in	10cm	4in
1cm	½in	15cm	6in
2cm	¾in	18cm	7in
2.5cm	1in	20.5cm	8in
3cm	1¼in	23cm	9in
4cm	1½in	25.5cm	10in
5cm	2in	28cm	11in
7.5cm	3in	30.5cm	12in

WEIGHTS

Metric	Imperial	Metric	Imperial
15g	½oz	275g	10oz
25g	1oz	300g	11oz
40g	1½oz	350g	12oz
50g	2oz	375g	13oz
75g	3oz	400g	14oz
100g	3½oz	425g	15oz
125g	4oz	450g	1lb
150g	5oz	550g	1¼lb
175g	6oz	700g	1½lb
200g	7oz	900g	2lb
225g	8oz	1.1kg	2½lb
250g	9oz		

Food safety & hygiene

- Always wash your hands before handling any food.
- Always wash fruit and vegetables before using them.
- Ensure your work surfaces and chopping boards are clean. Keep a separate chopping board for preparing raw meat.
- Cool leftover food as quickly as possible, ideally within one to two hours, and then store covered in the fridge.
- Leftover rice must be stored covered and for no longer than one day.
- Do not buy cracked eggs.
- If you are reheating food, make sure you heat all the way through and until it is piping hot. Do not reheat food more than once. Do not keep leftovers for longer than two days.
- Once thawed, do not refreeze raw food unless you have cooked it first.
- Read and follow the use-by dates on packaging and jars.
- Children, pregnant women or the elderly should not eat recipes that contain raw eggs.
- Ensure that your fridge is 5°C or less and the deep freeze is at least -20°C.
- Change and wash tea towels, towels, dishcloths, aprons and oven gloves often. Keep your pets away from surfaces and tables.
- Organise your fridge so that meat is kept separately and on the bottom shelf. Keep dairy produce together and fruit, vegetables and salad ingredients in the salad compartment.
- Store raw foods separately from cooked foods to avoid contamination.
- After shopping, put all food for the refrigerator and freezer into their allotted places as soon as possible.